GRAPHIC AMERICA

INVENTIONS AND INVENTORS

DARREN SECHRIST

Crabtree Publishing Company

www.crabtreebooks.com

Crabtree Publishing Company
www.crabtreebooks.com

Author:
Darren Sechrist
Coordinating editor:
Chester Fisher
Editors:
Scholastic Ventures Inc.
Molly Aloian
Copy editor:
Scholastic Ventures Inc.
Proofreaders:
Adrianna Morganelli
Crystal Sikkens
Project editor:
Robert Walker
Production coordinator:
Katherine Berti
Prepress technicians:
Ken Wright
Katherine Berti
Logo design:
Samantha Crabtree
Project manager:
Santosh Vasudevan (Q2AMedia)
Art direction:
Rahul Dhiman (Q2AMedia)
Design:
Tarang Saggar (Q2AMedia)
Illustrations:
Q2AMedia

Library and Archives Canada Cataloguing in Publication

Sechrist, Darren
Inventions and inventors / Darren Sechrist.

(Graphic America)
Includes index.
ISBN 978-0-7787-4186-2 (bound).--ISBN 978-0-7787-4213-5 (pbk.)

1. Inventions--United States--History--Comic books, strips, etc.--Juvenile literature. 2. Inventors--United States--History--Comic books, strips, etc.--Juvenile literature. I. Title. II. Series.

T21.S42 2008 j609.73 C2008-906399-6

Library of Congress Cataloging-in-Publication Data

Sechrist, Darren.
Inventions and inventors / Darren Sechrist.
p. cm. -- (Graphic America)
Includes index.
ISBN-13: 978-0-7787-4213-5 (pbk. : alk. paper)
ISBN-10: 0-7787-4213-X (pbk. : alk. paper)
ISBN-13: 978-0-7787-4186-2 (reinforced library binding : alk. paper)
ISBN-10: 0-7787-4186-9 (reinforced library binding : alk. paper)
1. Inventions--United States--History--Juvenile literature. 2. Inventors--United States--History--Juvenile literature. I. Title. II. Series.

T21.S42 2008
609.73--dc22

2008043037

Crabtree Publishing Company

Printed in Canada/092023/CPC20230901

www.crabtreebooks.com 1-800-387-7650
Copyright © **2009 CRABTREE PUBLISHING COMPANY**. All rights reserved. No part of this publication may be reproduced, stored in a retrieval system or be transmitted in any form or by any means, electronic, mechanical, photocopying, recording, or otherwise, without the prior written permission of Crabtree Publishing Company. In Canada: We acknowledge the financial support of the Government of Canada through the Canada Book Fund for our publishing activities.

Published in Canada
Crabtree Publishing
616 Welland Ave.
St. Catharines, ON
L2M 5V6

Published in the United States
Crabtree Publishing
347 Fifth Ave
Suite 1402-145
New York, NY 10016

Published in the United Kingdom
Crabtree Publishing
Maritime House
Basin Road North, Hove
BN41 1WR

Published in Australia
Crabtree Publishing
Unit 3-5
Currumbin Court
Capalaba QLD 4157

CONTENTS

BUILDING A BETTER WORLD

CHECK THIS OUT!

YOU CAN WATCH VIDEOS ON SOMETHING THAT FITS IN YOUR POCKET. YOU CAN USE A PHONE OR E-MAIL TO TALK TO SOMEONE ON THE OTHER SIDE OF THE WORLD. AIRPLANES AND CARS ALLOW US TO GET JUST ABOUT ANYWHERE. HOWEVER, LIFE WAS NOT ALWAYS THIS WAY.

JUST A FEW HUNDRED YEARS AGO, LIFE WAS MUCH HARDER. PEOPLE USED HORSES TO GET FROM PLACE TO PLACE. MAIL WAS THE ONLY WAY TO SEND MESSAGES. CANDLES WERE THE ONLY LIGHTS. WHEN THE SUN WENT DOWN, THE DAY WAS OVER.

THAT'S IT FOR TODAY. BACK AT IT TOMORROW.

DURING THE 1800S, THINGS CHANGED QUICKLY. PEOPLE WERE FINDING WAYS TO MAKE THINGS FASTER AND CHEAPER. PEOPLE WERE FINDING NEW WAYS TO DO OTHER THINGS, TOO.

THAT'S IT!

INVENTORS *PLAYED AN IMPORTANT PART IN THESE CHANGES. THEY FOUND NEW WAYS TO TRAVEL. THEY CAME UP WITH NEW WAYS TO SEND MESSAGES TO EACH OTHER. THEY EVEN FOUND A WAY TO LIGHT UP THE NIGHT.*

BENJAMIN FRANKLIN: AMERICA'S FIRST INVENTOR

THAT SHOULD KEEP ME WARM FOR THE NIGHT.

PEOPLE REMEMBER BENJAMIN FRANKLIN AS A FOUNDER OF THE UNITED STATES. HE WAS ALSO ITS FIRST GREAT INVENTOR. HE WORKED HARD EARLY IN HIS LIFE. BY THE TIME HE WAS FORTY YEARS OLD, HE HAD PLENTY OF MONEY. HE STARTED WORKING ON **INVENTIONS**. HIS FIRST INVENTION WAS THE FRANKLIN STOVE. THE STOVE WAS SAFER THAN THE FIREPLACES THAT PEOPLE HAD USED BEFORE. IT ALSO USED LESS FUEL.

FRANKLIN DID A LOT OF WORK WITH ELECTRICITY. ONCE, HE FLEW A KITE DURING A THUNDERSTORM. LIGHTNING HIT THE KITE AND ELECTRICITY MOVED DOWN THE STRING. IT MADE A SPARK ON A METAL KEY. THIS PROVED FRANKLIN'S IDEA THAT LIGHTNING WAS ELECTRICITY. HE USED WHAT HE LEARNED TO MAKE THE **LIGHTNING ROD**. IT ATTRACTS LIGHTNING AND SENDS THE ELECTRICITY INTO THE GROUND. THIS PREVENTS BUILDINGS FROM BEING STRUCK BY LIGHTNING.

YOU SEE? YOU SEE? IT IS ELECTRICITY!

THERE ARE THREE THINGS EXTREMELY HARD: STEEL, DIAMOND, AND TO KNOW ONE'S SELF.*
FRANKLIN HAD TROUBLE SEEING BOTH NEAR AND FAR. SO HE INVENTED A NEW PAIR OF GLASSES. THE UPPER PART OF EACH **LENS** LET HIM SEE FAR AWAY. THE LOWER PART MADE READING EASIER. THE GLASSES WERE CALLED **BIFOCALS**. MILLIONS OF PEOPLE STILL USE THEM TODAY.

FRANKLIN KEPT WORKING HARD INTO HIS OLD AGE. AT AGE 81, HE HELPED TO WRITE THE U.S. **CONSTITUTION**. IN A WAY, FRANKLIN HELPED TO INVENT A NEW COUNTRY: THE UNITED STATES!

* ACTUAL QUOTE

SAMUEL B. MORSE AND THE TELEGRAPH

STAY STILL. I'LL BE FINISHED SOON.
FOR MUCH OF HIS LIFE, SAMUEL B. MORSE WAS NOT AN INVENTOR. HE WORKED FOR MANY YEARS AS AN ARTIST AND TEACHER, BUT HE WAS ALWAYS INTERESTED IN **ELECTROMAGNETS**.

IN 1832, MORSE WAS ON A BOAT RIDE TALKING ABOUT ELECTRICITY WITH ANOTHER PASSENGER. SUDDENLY, HE HAD AN IDEA FOR A NEW WAY TO SEND MESSAGES. IT WOULD USE ELECTROMAGNETS. MESSAGES WOULD MOVE ALONG A WIRE AS ELECTRICITY. ON THE OTHER END, A PERSON WOULD GET THE MESSAGE IN SECONDS.
THEY ARE DOING MANY THINGS WITH ELECTRICITY IN PARIS. FOR ONE...
THAT GIVES ME AN IDEA. COULD IT REALLY WORK? I WONDER.

MORSE QUICKLY BEGAN WORKING ON HIS IDEA. BY 1838, HE HAD A WORKING MODEL. IT WAS CALLED A **TELEGRAPH**. IN 1843, A LINE BETWEEN WASHINGTON AND BALTIMORE WAS SET UP TO TEST MORSE'S INVENTION. ON MAY 24, 1844, MORSE TRIED SENDING A MESSAGE ON THE LINE. THE MESSAGE WAS RECEIVED RIGHT AWAY.

WHAT... HATH... GOD... WROUGHT!

BEFORE MORSE, THE ONLY WAY TO SEND MESSAGES WAS BY MAIL. THAT COULD TAKE MANY DAYS. WITH THE TELEGRAPH, IT TOOK ONLY SECONDS. BY 1861, WIRES STRETCHED ACROSS THE UNITED STATES. THANKS TO MORSE, MESSAGES MOVED QUICKER THAN EVER BEFORE.

THOMAS EDISON: LIGHTING UP THE WORLD

I JUST WANTED TO SEE WHAT WOULD HAPPEN.

*THOMAS EDISON WAS BORN IN OHIO IN 1847. HE LIKED TO TRY THINGS OUT TO SEE HOW THEY WORKED. AT THE AGE OF SIX, HE TRIED **EXPERIMENTING** WITH FIRE. HE ACCIDENTALLY BURNED DOWN HIS FAMILY'S BARN!*

EDISON WAS NOT MUCH OF A STUDENT. HE OFTEN DID NOT PAY ATTENTION IN CLASS. HE ALSO HAD TROUBLE HEARING, WHICH MADE SCHOOL EVEN HARDER. AFTER ONLY THREE MONTHS, HIS MOTHER PULLED HIM OUT OF SCHOOL. SHE DECIDED TO TEACH HIM HERSELF.
YOU'RE NOT GOING TO HAVE IT EASY HERE AT HOME. YOU'RE GOING TO READ ALL THE GREAT WORKS AND LEARN FROM THEM.

WHAT IS THAT NOISE DOWN THERE?
NOTHING, MOTHER.
AT HOME, EDISON LEARNED BY DOING. HE USED HIS FAMILY'S BASEMENT TO TRY ALL SORTS OF EXPERIMENTS. HE WORKED ON THE TELEGRAPH A LOT. HE EVEN MADE ONE OF HIS OWN.

WITH THIS MACHINE, YOU WILL HAVE UP-TO-THE-MINUTE PRICES.
IN 1868, EDISON BUILT A NEW KIND OF VOTING MACHINE. IT WAS HIS FIRST MAJOR INVENTION. SOON AFTER, HE CAME UP WITH A MACHINE THAT QUICKLY REPORTED GOLD PRICES.

IN 1876, EDISON MOVED TO MENLO PARK, NEW JERSEY. THERE, HE SET UP A HUGE FACTORY. THE FACTORY DID NOT MAKE CARS OR CLOTHES. IT WAS THE FIRST FACTORY THAT CREATED INVENTIONS.

I HAVE NEVER SEEN ANYTHING LIKE THIS. IT'S LIKE A FACTORY OF... IDEAS.

ONE YEAR LATER, EDISON INVENTED THE **PHONOGRAPH**. IT WAS A MACHINE THAT COULD RECORD SOUNDS AND PLAY THEM BACK.
MARY HAD A LITTLE LAMB...

I CALL THIS THE LIGHT BULB! IT WILL ALLOW YOU TO LIGHT YOUR HOME SAFELY AND CHEAPLY.
BEFORE EDISON, MOST PEOPLE HAD TO LIGHT THEIR HOUSES WITH CANDLES. IN 1879, EDISON CHANGED THAT. HE INVENTED THE ELECTRIC LIGHT BULB. IT ALLOWED PEOPLE TO USE ELECTRICITY TO LIGHT THEIR HOMES.

I NEVER DID A DAY'S WORK IN MY LIFE. IT WAS ALL FUN.*
EDISON KEPT WORKING HARD. HE FAILED MANY TIMES, BUT HE DID NOT GIVE UP. BY THE TIME HE DIED IN 1931, HE HAD MADE MORE THAN 1,000 INVENTIONS, THE MOST IN U.S. HISTORY.

* ACTUAL QUOTE

ALEXANDER GRAHAM BELL AND THE TELEPHONE

EVEN AS A BOY IN SCOTLAND, ALEXANDER GRAHAM BELL LIKED TO LEARN ABOUT SPEECH AND SOUND. HE STUDIED THE SUBJECTS WITH HIS FATHER AND GRANDFATHER. BELL EVEN TRIED TO TEACH HIS DOG TO TALK.

SAY 'HELLO.' 'HHHEEELLLOOO.'
RRRRRROOORRRR.

IN THE 1860S, WHEN BELL WAS A TEENAGER, HIS FATHER GAVE HIM A CHALLENGE. HE ASKED BELL AND HIS BROTHER TO BUILD A MACHINE THAT COULD TALK. THE BROTHERS WORKED FOR A LONG TIME. THEY FINALLY GOT THEIR MACHINE TO WORK. IT MADE A NOISE THAT SOUNDED LIKE A BABY SAYING "MAMA." THEY USED IT TO PLAY A JOKE ON THEIR NEIGHBORS.
GOOD GRACIOUS. WHAT CAN THE MATTER BE WITH THAT BABY?
MAMA. MAMA. MAMA.

MR. WATSON, COME HERE. I WANT TO SEE YOU.*

BELL MOVED TO THE UNITED STATES IN 1871. HE KEPT STUDYING VOICES AND SOUND. IN 1874, HE HAD AN IDEA FOR AN INVENTION CALLED A TELEPHONE. IT WOULD BE LIKE A TELEGRAPH, ONLY BETTER. HE THOUGHT HE COULD USE ELECTRICITY TO CARRY A VOICE LONG DISTANCES. HE WORKED ON THE TELEPHONE FOR TWO YEARS. ON MARCH 10, 1876, HE TRIED OUT HIS INVENTION. IT WORKED!

WITHIN A FEW YEARS, THOUSANDS OF TELEPHONES WERE BEING USED. BY THE 1950S, THEY WERE IN HOMES ACROSS AMERICA. TODAY PHONES OF ALL KINDS ARE USED MILLIONS OF TIMES EACH DAY.

YEAH. WE'RE MEETING AT CAROLINE'S. SEE YOU THERE.

GEORGE WASHINGTON CARVER: PLANT DOCTOR

GEORGE WASHINGTON CARVER WAS BORN IN 1864 AS A **SLAVE**. CARVER'S FATHER DIED AROUND THE TIME HE WAS BORN. WHEN HE WAS JUST A BABY, HE AND HIS MOTHER WERE KIDNAPPED. HIS MOTHER WAS NEVER FOUND, BUT CARVER WAS FOUND AND RETURNED TO THE FARM WHERE HE LIVED.

SO, PLANT DOCTOR, WHAT DO YOU THINK?
YOU ARE WATERING THEM TOO MUCH.

THE WHITE OWNERS OF THE FARM WHERE CARVER LIVED RAISED CARVER AND HIS BROTHER. IN 1865, SLAVES IN THE UNITED STATES WERE FREED. IN HIS EARLY LIFE, CARVER WAS WEAK AND COULD NOT DO MUCH WORK. HE SPENT A LOT OF HIS TIME STUDYING PLANTS AND GARDENING. HE EVEN HELPED NEIGHBORS WITH PLANTS THAT WERE SICK. THEY CALLED HIM THE "PLANT DOCTOR."

ONCE AGAIN, MR. CARVER HAS THE ANSWER FOR US.
AT AGE 12, CARVER STARTED GOING TO A SCHOOL FOR AFRICAN AMERICANS. HE WAS A VERY GOOD STUDENT. IN 1894, HE BECAME THE FIRST AFRICAN AMERICAN TO GRADUATE FROM IOWA STATE **AGRICULTURAL** COLLEGE. THERE HE LEARNED MORE ABOUT PLANTS AND FARMING. TWO YEARS LATER, HE EARNED A MASTER'S DEGREE.

IN 1896, CARVER MOVED ON TO A NEW AFRICAN AMERICAN SCHOOL IN ALABAMA. IT WAS CALLED THE TUSKEGEE INSTITUTE. CARVER TAUGHT CLASSES ON PLANTS AND FARMING. HE ALSO DID EXPERIMENTS WITH PLANTS.

CARVER WANTED TO HELP AFRICAN AMERICANS HAVE BETTER LIVES. MANY AFRICAN AMERICANS RAISED COTTON PLANTS, BUT COTTON WAS BAD FOR THE SOIL. CARVER LOOKED FOR A WAY TO MAKE THE SOIL RICH AND HEALTHY AGAIN.
THE CROP'S SMALLER THAN LAST YEAR.
THERE'S LESS EVERY YEAR. IT'S THIS SOIL.

I'VE NEVER SEEN COTTON GROW LIKE THIS.
YES, BUT WHAT WILL WE DO WITH PEANUTS?
IN HIS RESEARCH, CARVER MADE AN AMAZING DISCOVERY. HE FOUND THAT PEANUTS AND SWEET POTATOES MADE THE SOIL RICHER. HE TAUGHT FARMERS TO PLANT THESE CROPS. THIS HELPED MAKE THE SOIL HEALTHY.

IT IS MADE FROM PEANUTS. SO THIS BUTTER IS HIGH IN PROTEIN.
AND IT TASTES GOOD, TOO!
CARVER DID NOT JUST TELL PEOPLE WHAT TO GROW. HE ALSO TOLD THEM HOW TO USE THEIR NEW CROPS. HE FOUND WAYS TO MAKE PEANUTS INTO BUTTERS, MEDICINES, AND OTHER USEFUL THINGS. HE SHOWED PEOPLE HOW TO MAKE GLUES AND **DYES** FROM SWEET POTATOES.

KNOW SCIENCE, AND SCIENCE SHALL SET YOU FREE...*
CARVER SPENT MORE THAN 50 YEARS AT TUSKEGEE. HE RECEIVED MANY AWARDS FOR HIS WORK. HE DISCOVERED MORE THAN 300 USES FOR PEANUTS AND SWEET POTATOES. BUT HE NEVER TRIED TO MAKE MONEY OFF OF HIS WORK. HE SHARED HIS IDEAS TO HELP AFRICAN AMERICANS.

HENRY FORD AND THE CAR

ARE YOU SURE YOU KNOW WHAT YOU ARE DOING?
IT WILL BE FIXED IN A MOMENT.
AS A KID, HENRY FORD LOVED MACHINES. AT HIS FAMILY'S FARM IN DEARBORN, MICHIGAN, HE LIKED TO TAKE APART TOYS AND WATCHES TO SEE HOW THEY WORKED. HE LEARNED A GREAT DEAL. SOON, HE WAS FIXING WATCHES FOR NEIGHBORS AND FRIENDS.

WHEN HE WAS A TEENAGER, FORD SAW A STEAM ENGINE ROLLING DOWN THE ROAD. HE FELL IN LOVE WITH THE MACHINE. ITS GEARS AND CHAINS REMINDED HIM OF A WATCH. HE DECIDED HE WOULD BUILD ONE SOME DAY.
FATHER, LOOK! THE GEARS MOVE AND MAKE IT WORK, JUST LIKE A WATCH. IT'S AMAZING!

AS AN ADULT, FORD STARTED BUILDING HIS OWN MACHINE. HE CALLED IT A "QUADRACYCLE." IT WOULD RUN ON GAS, NOT STEAM. IN 1893, HE TOLD THOMAS EDISON ABOUT HIS PLANS. EDISON THOUGHT IT WAS A GREAT IDEA. HE TOLD FORD TO KEEP WORKING.

YOUR CAR IS SELF-CONTAINED...CARRIES ITS OWN POWER PLANT...NO FIRE, NO BOILER, NO SMOKE, AND NO STEAM. YOU HAVE THE THING. KEEP AT IT!*

SHE'S BEAUTIFUL, HENRY!
FORD KEPT AT IT. HE WORKED ON HIS QUADRACYCLE FOR THREE MORE YEARS. IN 1896, HE FINALLY FINISHED. IT LOOKED LIKE A CARRIAGE WITHOUT HORSES. IT WAS STEERED WITH A STICK. ONE NIGHT, HE AND A FRIEND TOOK IT FOR A TEST DRIVE.

BY THE EARLY 1900S, OTHER PEOPLE HAD STARTED BUILDING CARS, TOO. FORD WANTED TO PROVE THAT HIS CARS WERE THE BEST. IN 1901, HE BEGAN RACING HIS CARS. FORD'S CARS WON RACES AGAINST OTHER TOP CARS. FORD AND HIS CARS SOON BECAME FAMOUS.

I CANNOT KEEP UP.
YOU WILL GET THE HANG OF IT.

A FEW YEARS LATER, FORD BEGAN MAKING CARS TO SELL TO THE PUBLIC. HIS FIRST MODELS SOLD WELL. BUT FORD STILL THOUGHT HE COULD FIND A WAY TO MAKE CARS CHEAPER AND BETTER. HE CAME UP WITH THE IDEA OF AN **ASSEMBLY LINE**. PIECES OF THE CAR WOULD MOVE ALONG ON A BELT. EACH WORKER WOULD DO THE SAME JOB OVER AND OVER. FORD ALSO KEPT HIS WORKERS HAPPY WITH SHORTER HOURS AND HIGHER PAY.

CARS ARE NOT JUST FOR THE RICH ANYMORE. THE MODEL T IS ONLY $550!
THE ASSEMBLY LINE MADE THE WORK MUCH FASTER. LESS TIME WAS WASTED AND MORE CARS COULD BE BUILT EACH DAY. IN 1908, FORD STARTED SELLING THE MODEL T FOR $550. THAT WAS FAR LESS THAN OTHER CARS COST. MANY FAMILIES DID NOT HAVE ENOUGH MONEY FOR OTHER CARS, BUT THEY HAD ENOUGH FOR A MODEL T.

MORE THAN 15 MILLION MODEL TS WERE SOLD IN ALL. CARS QUICKLY BECAME A PART OF THE AMERICAN WAY OF LIFE. MANY COMPANIES COPIED FORD'S ASSEMBLY LINE PLAN. IT HELPED BUSINESSES AROUND THE WORLD WORK FASTER AND BETTER.

GUGLIELMO MARCONI AND THE WIRELESS WORLD

GUGLIELMO MARCONI WAS BORN IN ITALY IN 1874. INSTEAD OF GOING TO SCHOOL, HE LEARNED AT HOME. MARCONI SPENT A LOT OF TIME READING. HE ALSO DID MANY EXPERIMENTS WITH ELECTRICITY.
THE MESSAGE TRAVELS THROUGH THE AIR? NO WIRES?
AT AGE 20, MARCONI READ ABOUT THE WORK OF HEINRICH HERTZ. HERTZ HAD DONE WORK WITH INVISIBLE ENERGY CALLED RADIO WAVES. MARCONI THOUGHT HE COULD USE THE WAVES TO SEND TELEGRAPH MESSAGES. HE SET UP EXPERIMENTS IN HIS FATHER'S GARDEN. SOON, HE WAS SENDING MESSAGES OVER A MILE AWAY WITHOUT WIRES.

SIR, THEY HAVE FOUND THE ENEMY SHIP.
MARCONI MOVED TO ENGLAND IN 1896. HE STARTED HIS OWN WIRELESS TELEGRAPH BUSINESS. IN 1899, MARCONI WAS ABLE TO SEND WIRELESS MESSAGES FROM ENGLAND TO FRANCE. IN 1901, HE SENT A TELEGRAPH MESSAGE FROM THE UNITED STATES ALL THE WAY ACROSS THE ATLANTIC OCEAN. RADIO, AS IT WAS CALLED, SOON BECAME THE WAY FOR SHIPS TO SEND AND RECEIVE MESSAGES.
GREAT SONG. TURN IT UP!
TODAY, RADIO IS STILL USED TO SEND MESSAGES BACK AND FORTH. BUT IT IS USED IN OTHER WAYS, TOO. RADIO STATIONS AROUND THE WORLD USE IT TO BROADCAST MUSIC AND NEWS.

FIRST IN FLIGHT: THE WRIGHT BROTHERS

I COULD USE YOUR HELP, BROTHER.
JUST A MOMENT. I THINK I HAVE FIGURED SOMETHING OUT.
ORVILLE AND WILBUR WRIGHT RAN A BICYCLE SHOP. BUT THE TWO BROTHERS WERE MORE INTERESTED IN FLYING THAN IN RIDING. THEY READ EVERYTHING THAT THEY COULD FIND ON THE SUBJECT. THEY LEARNED EVEN MORE BY EXPERIMENTING WITH BOX KITES.

SOON, ORVILLE AND WILBUR STARTED MAKING **GLIDERS**. THESE ALLOWED A PERSON TO FLY USING ONLY THE POWER OF THE WIND. BUT THE BROTHERS FOUND THAT STEERING GLIDERS WAS NOT EASY. MANY OF THEIR EARLY ATTEMPTS TO FLY FAILED.
TURN TO THE RIGHT. THE RIGHT!
I AM!

ORVILLE AND WILBUR WERE STUMPED. HOW COULD THEY MAKE THEIR FLYING MACHINES EASIER TO STEER? ONE DAY, THEY NOTICED THAT BIRDS COULD BEND THE TIPS OF THEIR WINGS. MAYBE THIS GAVE THE BIRDS MORE CONTROL. THEY DECIDED TO TRY IT WITH THEIR GLIDERS. BENDING THE WINGS WORKED LIKE A CHARM.

IT'S WORKING!
GOOD. WATCH OUT FOR TREES!

FOR YEARS, THE BROTHERS KEPT TESTING THEIR GLIDER. THEY KEPT MAKING IMPROVEMENTS. IN 1903, THEY ADDED AN ENGINE TO THEIR INVENTION. ON DECEMBER 17, 1903, THE BROTHERS TESTED THEIR ENGINE-POWERED GLIDER IN KITTY HAWK, NORTH CAROLINA. ORVILLE FLEW 120 FEET IN 12 SECONDS. THE WRIGHT BROTHERS HAD INVENTED AN AIRPLANE!

WE HAVE DONE IT! WE CAN FLY!

TIMELINE

1787 – BENJAMIN FRANKLIN AND OTHER FOUNDING FATHERS MEET IN PHILADELPHIA TO WRITE THE U.S. CONSTITUTION.

1838 – SAMUEL B. MORSE COMPLETES A WORKING MODEL OF THE TELEGRAPH.

1868 – THOMAS EDISON CREATES THE FIRST OF HIS MANY INVENTIONS—A NEW TYPE OF VOTING MACHINE.

1876 – ALEXANDER GRAHAM BELL IMPROVES THE TELEGRAPH BY INVENTING THE TELEPHONE.

1879 – THOMAS EDISON INVENTS THE LIGHT BULB, PROVIDING A SAFE WAY FOR PEOPLE TO LIGHT THEIR HOMES.

1896 – GEORGE WASHINGTON CARVER JOINS THE TUSKEGEE INSTITUTE, WHERE HE SPENDS THE NEXT 50 YEARS STUDYING AND TEACHING ABOUT PLANTS.

1900 – GUGLIELMO MARCONI PATENTED HIS FIRST RADIO.

1903 – THE WRIGHT BROTHERS COMPLETE THE FIRST SUCCESSFUL FLIGHT OF AN AIRPLANE.

1908 – HENRY FORD INTRODUCES THE MODEL T, ONE OF THE MOST SUCCESSFUL CARS OF ALL TIME.

GLOSSARY

AGRICULTURAL HAVING TO DO WITH THE SCIENCE OF GROWING CROPS AND RAISING ANIMALS

ASSEMBLY LINE A LINE OF MACHINES THAT BUILDS SOMETHING ONE PIECE AT A TIME

BIFOCALS EYEGLASSES THAT CORRECT VISION TO SEE BOTH NEAR AND FAR-AWAY OBJECTS

CHALLENGE AN OFFER OR A DARE TO DO SOMETHING

CONSTITUTION A DOCUMENT THAT EXPLAINS A NATION'S RULES AND LAWS

DYE SOMETHING USED TO COLOR CLOTHING AND OTHER FABRICS

ELECTROMAGNET MAGNETS WRAPPED WITH WIRE THAT HAVE ELECTRICITY RUNNING THROUGH THEM

EXPERIMENT TESTS USED TO SEE HOW SOMETHING, SUCH AS AN INVENTION, WORKS

GLIDER A KIND OF AIRPLANE THAT DOES NOT HAVE AN ENGINE

INVENTION A PRODUCT OR IDEA THAT IS NEW OR DIFFERENT FROM ANYTHING CREATED BEFORE IT

INVENTOR THE FIRST PERSON TO CREATE A PRODUCT OR IDEA

LENS SPECIAL GLASS USED IN EYEGLASSES TO IMPROVE VISION

LIGHTNING ROD A METAL ROD CONNECTED WITH THE EARTH TO PREVENT A BUILDING FROM GETTING HIT BY LIGHTNING

PATENT A DOCUMENT THAT PREVENTS OTHER PEOPLE FROM COPYING AN INVENTOR'S IDEA FOR A CERTAIN PERIOD OF TIME.

PHONOGRAPH A MACHINE THAT CAN RECORD AND PLAY BACK SOUND

SLAVE A SERVANT WHO IS OWNED BY ANOTHER PERSON

TELEGRAPH A MACHINE USED TO SEND MESSAGES OVER A WIRE

INDEX

WEBFINDER

HTTP://WWW.FI.EDU/FRANKLIN/

HTTP://WWW.ALEXANDERGRAHAMBELL.ORG/

HTTP://WWW.INVENT.ORG/HALL_OF_FAME/1_0_0_HALL_OF_FAME.ASP

HTTP://WWW.NPS.GOV/HISTORY/MUSEUM/EXHIBITS/TUSKEGEE/GWCOVERVIEW.HTM

HTTP://WWW.NASM.SI.EDU/WRIGHTBROTHERS/INDEX_FULL.CFM